How to Start a Publishing Company

Turn Your Passion into Profit Using This Comprehensive Publishing Business Blueprint

By

Maxwell Rotheray

1

Table of Contents

Introduction

I f you are an author, or you want to be an author or you just want to publish other people's work, starting your own publishing business is a great leap towards realizing your dream.

For many people, establishing your business can be bewildering, mind-numbing, and a very difficult task.

Fortunately, the steps in this book have been put forward as a guide and hopefully to help you find out if you should start a publishing company and the necessary steps for you to take.

In this edition, you will gain knowledge of:

Step One: Determine your business structure

Step Two: Choose a Business Name

Step Three: Pick Where to Locate Your Business

Step Four: Register Your Business

Step Five: Legalize Your Business

Step Six: Managing Your Publishing Business

CHAPTER 1: Publishing Companies Abound

Some book publishing houses specialize in different types of publications depending on the market the books are meant to serve. Below are some of the publishers with varieties of publications.

1. Trade Book Publishers

These publishers procure, prepare for publication, create, print, and market books you normally see in brick-and-mortar bookstores. They are the established publishers producing books for the vast majority of consumer readership.

2. Book Packagers and Book Developers

Book packagers are publishers who specialize in developing books to be published under the banner of a trade publisher. The book packager creates a concept for a book and then sells the idea to a publisher. The packager is responsible for the editorial and production of the book on behalf of the publisher. When the books are eventually published, they are shipped to the publisher's warehouse.

3. "Bargain" Book Publishers

These publishers are into creating low-cost books and book-related products like diaries and calendars.

4. Textbook Publishers and Academic Publishers

Textbook publishers develop books for teaching purposes in colleges and universities, usually with a specific course curriculum in view. There are so many publishers in this category out there such as McGraw-Hill, Houghton Mifflin, Pearson, etc.

5. Professional Publishers

Professional publishers are responsible for creating books and databases for professionals such as doctors, accountants, lawyers, etc., who always need pertinent, reliable, information and standards.

6. Vanity, Self and Contract Publishers

Vanity and contract publishers create and print books under speciality contracts. The cost of publication is borne by Individual authors and companies. These publishers undertake to publish books and charge fees for their services.

7. Electronic Books

Electronic book publishing gives readers access to read and download the text online or buy digital books from retail stores.

CHAPTER 2: The Reasons for You to Start a Publishing Business

B efore we go into the process proper of setting up a publishing business, let's, first of all, find out why someone should be into it.

If we consider today's publishing platform, it might not be necessary to start your own publishing business to publish your work or the work of others. However, it is beneficial to do so for the following reasons:

- It shows you are a professional and an expert in your field.

- It gives your work, yourself and your assets legal protection in the event of litigation.

- You have full control in managing your intellectual property

- There is perpetual succession.

- There are special tax rebates.

- You maintain control over your work

- You have access to more than one Amazon KDP account (and still within Amazon's TOS)

- You have the opportunity of becoming an entrepreneur instead of a hobby writer.

- Makes you realize your dream of being The Boss/CEO/Founder of your own publishing business

- Opportunity to publish works of other authors

From the foregoing, you can see the numerous advantages to starting a publishing business. Next, we'll go into the nitty-gritty of some of those advantages and probably explore them in greater detail. This will help you determine if this is the opportune moment for you to go into the publishing business.

CHAPTER 3: Benefits of Starting a Publishing Business

1) Protect Yourself and Your Asset

Although it doesn't happen all the time, slightest libel or slander can trigger lawsuits and when it happens, can last for a long time. If you don't have a limited liability company in place, and your publication gets sued, then your finances and the public record will be a major risk, you may be in for a long bitter battle.

Having a registered company confers on you legal protection and helps to separate your business finances and your finances. The courts, or other collection agencies, wouldn't have rights over you your business assets.

2) Tax Breaks, Write-Offs, And Wealth Building

It doesn't matter which business structure you decide to have, putting in place your own publishing company can make it possible for you to write off certain business expenses, which are deductible as tax depending on your tax liability

Moreover, starting your publishing business also helps you separate your income and business revenue. This makes life much easier during the time of filing your tax returns, and with the new tax laws, it can deliver a lower tax liability.

3) Upgrade Your KDP Accounts

Moreover, another positive reason of starting a publishing company is that you'll have the opportunity to open a second Amazon KDP account.

The usual Amazon's Terms of Service (TOS) is that you can only have one KDP account.

But, one of the benefits of owning your own publishing company is that your company is entitled to have its own EIN and bank account, which makes it possible to have its KDP account and is therefore in line with the Terms of Service of Amazon. As it stands, you are entitled to have two accounts, the publishing account inclusive, which is available with added advantages of enlarged author's pages via author central, and therefore the use of more pen names.

4) Writing in Partnership with Other Authors and Obtaining a License

Having your publishing business, is an added advantage of having to co-write with another author and an added opportunity of publishing other author's book for them. Having your own publishing company is in no doubt the definite route to contracting with other authors, and consequently having a binding and lawful operating agreement. Being the owner of a publishing business, an opportunity has been presented to you to take advantage of future licensing and contracting opportunities.

CHAPTER 4: How to Start Your Publishing Outfit

Now that you have decided to go into the publishing business, here is the step by step approach of creating your own company and make it grow into an empire.

Step 1. Decide On a Business Structure

Before launching into a publishing business proper, you must decide which type of business structure you want to create.

Different types of businesses abound such as S-Corporations, Sole Proprietorship, General Partnership, Limited Liability Companies and others. Each one has its pros and cons.

In summary:

1.   S-Corporation

2.   The sole proprietorship

3.   General Partnership

4.   Registered companies

5.   Public enterprise

    1. **S Corporation** – by its nature, it satisfies the requirements of the

24

Internal Revenue as it can be assessed as a partnership for tax purposes. The requirements give the corporation with 100 shareholders or less the benefit of incorporation while being taxed as a partnership.

2. The sole proprietorship

It is an incorporated business, owned, managed and operated by one person

Attributes

1.   The ownership is vested in one person

2.   It is relatively small in size

3.   Control is not separated from ownership

4. The capital is usually small and generally provided by the owner-manager

5.   The true identity – it is identified with the owner.

Merits

1. Small capital requirements.

2. Operational autonomy and flexibility

3. Simplicity of organization

4. Effective management

5. The sole owner takes all the profit.

6. Privacy is guaranteed

7. Easy to dissolve

Demerits

1. Financial limitations

2. Unlimited liability

3. Managerial limitation

4. Possibility of discontinuity

5. Limitation on economies of scale

3. Partnership

An association of two or more individuals set up to carry on a business in common to make a profit.

A partnership agreement or deed is usually entered into by all partners concerned and it is this agreement that regulates all matters affecting the business and the relationship of the partners and the outside world.

Merits of partnership

1. An easy source of funds

2.   Privacy

3.   Joint decisions

4.   Division of labour

5.   Possibility of mass production

Demerits

1.   Not a legal entity

2.   Insufficient capital

3.   Unsure of continuity

27

4.   Prone to anarchy

5.   Delay of policy

6.   Unlimited liability – even there is one or two limited partners

4. Limited Liability Company

Attributes of limited liability companies

1.   Separate entity

2.   Limited liability of members

3.   Interests are transferable

4.   Perpetual succession

5. Members, not agents – directors and shareholders are not agents, unlike partnership.

Types of limited liability companies

1.   Private limited liability company.

2.   Public limited liability company

Private limited liability company is that in which:

(a) There are relatively few members to form the company.

(b)   No public subscription of shares

(c)   No right to transfer shares

(d)   Account not published

A public limited company is that which:

(a)   Many members can form a company.

(b)   Funds generated through public subscription

(c)   Ownership is divorced from management

(d)   Annual accounts are audited and published

(e)   Directors required to declare their interests in the company.

By and large "The Limited Liability Company should be the preferred structure to pick since it is by far the more flexible structure on how ownership and profit distribution is organized. The controlling document is known as an operating agreement and you can write up the agreement in whatever way you choose, fashioning out rules on how money is received and how it is expended. You can also fashion out rules for continuity, should you become incapacitated in running the business. A corporation is far more inflexible in its rules of operation than a Limited Liability Company. This is because there are stakeholders' holding company's shares, executive and non-executive directors, other officers, and the company internal rules regulating the company activities.

A Limited Liability Company has an added advantage which permits it to be assessed for tax purposes as a Sole Proprietorship, Partnership, or S-Corporation. Fundamentally, it is the best choice in this circumstance as it fits properly in the self-publishing business structure.

If you want to be double sure, you can verify this assertion from the evidence available from the vast majority of your favourite authority authors or bloggers and you will be convinced.

Step 2. Choose A Business Name

There is no hard and fast rule in selecting a publishing business name. You can choose a name that reflects your name or your genre, such as " Chrison Publications" or City Press".

Legally the name of your publishing business doesn't have to match up with the name of your actual business, it is possible to cause problems if they are dissimilar, anyway..

There are however 3 things you will have to consider before you make up your mind which business name you want to use.

1. Make sure the name is not registered as trademark elsewhere.

2. Never use the words "corporation" or "inc." if you register your publishing business as LLC because they mean entirely different.

3. Make sure the name isn't already taken by another company in your state if you reside in the U.S.

It is advisable to have alternative names handy should you be notified that the name you presented has been taken.

The good thing, however, is that the name availability is specific for a particular state, which means that even though a company may have a particular name in a state, if it hasn't been registered in the state you want to operate, then it is available.

The way to find out if your company name is taken is to go to your respective state's name search, using Google for this exercise.

Step 3. Choose A Location

It is important that in setting up the business, you need to differentiate between the State the business is registered, and the actual place you do your business.

The State The Business Is Registered

All States dish out articles to the organization for LLCs, so the first step in selecting a location in the state of the organization.

Now, you should be on your guard of those thrifty business people who are bent on looking for tax breaks or lower annual registration costs, you may have heard about business registration in states like Wyoming and Nevada.

A word of warning: Your state of abode and likely do most of your work expects to receive income tax from you. If you live and work in California for example, establishing your LLC in Nevada doesn't get you out of the tax net in California. Incorporating your business out of the state of abode can cost you more money since most states would like you to register "foreign entities" if you are to legally operate in the state. As far as California is concerned, for that Nevada business to operate legally in California it has to be registered in California. But, not all states are as money-conscious as California, so this is a question of which state.

Since the decision of which state you register your business has a long term cost implication, make sure you research before making up your mind.

Location of the Business

At the time of establishing an LLC, some self-publishers would prefer to use their home as their official location for their business since they must have a physical office place and not only office space for their business. However, this can cause a problem as well as being a potential for mistakes.

Be clear that your business address must be a physical location where legal documents can be handed out. With this requirement, the information you provide will be seen by members of the public. In some of the states, the owner's name will remain confidential; in its place is a registered agent that remains on the public record. You can choose to be your registered agent in almost all the states but your name will be displayed on a public record together with your address.

Consequently, if you decide to choose your place of abode as your business address, this places your personal information accessible to all and sundry and can violate your personal life.

So, what can you do to get out of this? Four options are available.

Rent a Physical Location: This option is very costly since the cost of renting an office is on the high side and can't be afforded by most business starters.

Get a UPS Mailbox: It makes business sense to procure a UPS mailbox since most states do not let you put a P.O. Box number on the application. Fortunately, UPS lets you have a mailbox that looks a lot like a regular address. By selecting this option, you are expected to be physically present to enable you to set up your mailbox. In essence, the state in which you choose to set up your LLC will be completely dependent on your ability to be physically present. However, once the mailbox has been set up, your mails can be forwarded to your real address.

Use A Registered Agent: Registered agent can handle this service for you but you must be ready to foot the bill for this service. The fee payable includes setting up your LLC. Using this service will eliminate your name since the registered agent is a public record.

Set up a Virtual Office: Virtual Offices appear the best option. These offices are professionally carried out as you get a specific mailing address, and get your mails forwarded to you as they arrive. Moreover, most virtual offices will give you a 1-800 number as well as record and dispatch your voice mail electronically. This option makes economic sense for those of you who are always travelling or living in a state that has high business taxes. Finally, you don't have to go in person to set it up. You can do it remotely from the comfort of your home in a different state, or a different country.

Step 4. Register Your Business

Having chosen LLC, the procedure for business registration is straight forward. You can choose to have a virtual office and empower them to sign corporate documents for you.

The cost of registration can vary from state to state but, invariably, the lowest fees are $50 while the highest is $800. In addition to the annual dues payable every year, if you choose to make use of a registered agent, there are supplementary fees payable as a result of the extra services. The fees authors pay range between $200-$500 a year.

Step 5: Actions to Be Taken to Become a Legitimate Business

Now that you've gone through the government hurdle, it's time to take certain steps to establish yourself as a legitimate business. There are couples of things you need to do to legitimize your Publishing Company.

Set up a Business Bank Account: Opening a business bank account is necessary in order to distinguish your personal bank account from your business bank account.

Obtain Your EIN and Update Accounts: Having a business in place, you'll obtain an EIN (an EIN resembles a Social Security number for businesses). Having obtained an EIN, ensure full documentation for any accounts that you have set up in the past.

Create a Publisher's KDP Account on Amazon: If you've works published in the past under your account and you decide to have them in your business account, you can change your account to your business account. You can do this by changing the essential information in your settings to reflect the business account such as your address and EIN. Alternatively, you can set up a new business account and move your books to it since Amazon's TOS doesn't allow two accounts.

Plan Your First Annual Business Meeting and Document It: As an LLC or even a corporation, you will have one annual business meeting in a year and ensure you take the minutes of the meeting. Failure to comply with this requirement will make you not to be seen as an LLC and your legitimacy diminishes.

Find Authors to Publish: You have now overcome all the hurdles and on the same pedestal with other fully-fledged publishing companies. To launch into the field to find good authors and publish their works and split royalty.

Step 6: How to Payout Royalties to Your Authors

If your new publishing company plans to manage co-authored works, you'll have an extra work of splitting royalties and dividends and pay to your authors. Splitting the royalties outstanding can pose a lot of problems, but never mind; **PublishDrive Abacus** has simplified the process of doing the calculation.

PublishDriveAbacus is a software that has brought a solution to the calculation of royalties and its essential features are as follows:

- It simplifies the calculation of royalties between co-authors

- It generates reports for each contributor.

- It makes the entire accounting process more efficient.

However, this program is designed for publishers that publish on Amazon and Kindle Unlimited. And I can bet you, it's very easy to use and you can use it.

CHAPTER 5: Why Publishing Business Can Be Profitable - Expected Profit

When compared with other industries, the book industry is doing pretty well in terms of profit margin. In a recent analysis done by industry publication, Publishers Lunch, the largest worldwide book publisher made about 10% profit margin. When compared to other industries, the profit margin of 10% was about right.

Profit in the analysis represents income after you have subtracted the following:

Editing of the publication

Proofreading

Cover design

ISBN registration

Formatting

Uploading to the chosen distributors.

Publishing Business Checklist

Whether you're a novice to the publishing process or an old-timer, it is important to have a checklist to guide your self-publishing project from start to finish, to guarantee you don't miss any vital stage in the process, as well as help you plan well enough not to miss your publication date.

In this e-book, we have detailed below the different stages of the editorial, production, and sales/marketing process. We aim to lend a hand to your understanding of some of the suppositions we've made about the publishing process. It is a simple traditional model but can save you time and expense.

CHAPTER 6: The Editorial and Production Process

This process can be split into three stages:

1. Editing
2. Design
3. Proofing

1. Editing

Our checklist starts at the stage where you have the final manuscript that has been reasonably edited and doesn't require advanced level editing or major revision. However, in most cases, it all depends on what level of editing your manuscript has gotten to and how much editing is still required. For most authors, we wouldn't hesitate to suggest seeking a formal copyedit: this means that you contract the services of a professional freelance copyeditor, who will work on the style, grammar, and consistency concerns of the manuscript.

A usual copyedit for a 100,000-word manuscript is edited for about two weeks, but good copyeditors typically need to be contacted ahead of time, up to a month or more in advance. Authors should earmark at least a week to two, to appraise and make changes where necessary after the copyedit has come back.

2. Design

Depending on your project, designers typically takes several stages to come up to a reasonably good design.

Front cover design. This is typically done simultaneously as the manuscript is being copyedited, beginning on the cover design. Some authors can come up with their cover designs with the help of Canva software, but since your cover page promotes your publication, it is advisable to hire a professional designer who is likely to do a better job

But before you begin to look for a cover designer, check out other bestselling books to your genre, theme, or audience and compare the covers. With this creative brief to your professional freelance designer, it is more likely they will do a fantastic job of designing the cover.

The title is also important, so if you haven't already done so you should work on the title, subtitle, and what describes the book which should be used at all retailer stores and also on the back cover (for the hard copy edition). It saves time and energy if you have up to two or three versions of what describes the book: a long one (25–50 words), a longer one (50–100 words), and the longest one (250 words).

Moreover, it's advisable to produce a front cover for your book well before the editing is done; all that remains is the final title/subtitle, a final assessment on your book's trim size, and is re-assured on what the cover should look like.

Back cover design. Typical eBooks only have a front cover design and without a back cover design. If you're printing a paperback or print-on-demand edition, then you must need a back cover and spine.

Conventional publishers normally produce the front cover design first, and they continue working on the back cover and spine well to the publication date. The spine is typically delayed until the exact page count is known unless the page count is firm and remains unchanged.

Print interior design. If you decide on a print edition *and* you can afford the time and money, you may also go for a designer to work on the interior of your book. This could be or not be the same designer of the cover, but it all depends on the skill set of the freelancer. Here are some of the things you consider before deciding if the interior designer is what you can employ.

- Books that are principally body text only (such as novels and memoirs), often fits well with very basic or template designs. It is possible for you to use the free Book Design Templates available on the web which are relatively inexpensive software to produce a good-looking print interior, perhaps with the help of Microsoft Word or InDesign. The same templates can also be used to create your e-book files. The use of a template system can reduce significantly the amount of time needed for book production.

- Books that are professionally designed especially non-fiction should require a custom-made interior design. This is so especially if you have images, illustrations, or any colour designs, you'll want to hire a designer who will have no difficulties setting up the file and ensuring quality reproduction.

- Whenever you decide to use InDesign in the production of both a print and a e-book editions, always be certain that both editions have the same final text since InDesign are not usually an easy process.

- If you must go for InDesign, you can hire an independent e-book formatting professional to do it for you.

Typically, before the process of interior design begins, the author lists out all the design elements that occur in the book. It may resemble something like this:

Chapter   title
A   head
B   head
Numbered list
Bulleted   list
Block quote

If you have difficulty coming up with a list like this, your designer should be able to assist you in this regard.

3. Proofing

When the design is complete, you'll have to make up your mind how deep your proofing process will be. Some authors proofread their files on their own, and others send them out for a formal proofread by professional freelancers. If your files are relatively clean and only very few errors have been brought in during the production process, then you might save the cost of hiring someone.

CHAPTER 7: The Sales and Distribution Process

This process typically has two stages:

1. Getting ready your metadata

2. Uploading your files and putting them out on sale

1. Preparing Your Metadata

Before you approach Ingram or Amazon to publish your book, it's a good idea to have the following handy: the description of your book, how it will be categorized, and your pricing method to adopt, and so on. That way, when you get at the publishing interface, you'll not be at a loss with all the pertinent information.

2. Sending your files for publication

This is the final stage where your files are offered for sale. Typically, your files don't take a lot of time to get into the system; in fact we estimate less than an hour to get your book into the system and therefore under review. If it happens you use Amazon for the sale, your book is likely to go for sale in less than twenty-four hours. If however, you are not ready to go on sale, then it is possible to set the book as a preorder and include whatever publication date you choose. (Amazon agrees on preorders up to ninety days in advance; others allow for one year.)

The under mentioned items should be handy at the time you decide to upload your print-on-demand edition:

- Full over outline file, should you prefer to work with both Amazon KDP and IngramSpark.

- Complete inside design file (PDF)

Moreover, the following files should be available for upload if you are going for an e-book edition:

- Frontage cover photo: any image formats can do,

- E-book file: EPUB will give you the best quality, but most retailers/distributors accept a Word document, among other common file formats

What's Not Included in This Checklist?

This checklist covers most of the steps concerned in creating your book and pushing it to the market place. But, it does not talk on any marketing issues, such as sending out advance review copies, the use of social media before release or afterwards, gathering endorsements, marketing a preorder, etc.

CHAPTER 8: How to Target the Right Customer

Your publishing company cannot serve everyone and satisfy their reading needs. A niche of the market should be earmarked and be pursued with tested promotional tools. You must spend time and resources gathering and analysing data about your potential readers' habits and motivations. It is an enormous task but it has to be done if you are going to make headway. The following are the steps recommended for you to target potential readers for your book publication.

1. **Survey your potential readers**

   Decide on the target audience you want to serve and deploy resources gathering and analyzing data about their reading habits and motivations. The purpose of the survey is to enable you to find out how you can better present your product and what aspect of your product might be currently missing and need to be fixed up before presenting it to your target market.

Expand your market within and outside your geographical area to include those you feel might be interested in your publication and use their data to streamline your brand in such a way that will satisfy the needs of your target market.

2. **Research your competitors to find out who their readers are**

To find out which marketing blitz should work for you and which one doesn't is by researching competitors in your industry. This is customarily an inexpensive effort but could reveal some awesome information to work with as well as revealing dark spots in your competitor's marketing process you should plan to avoid.

When you set up a publishing company, you are going after some of your competitors' target customers, so why not use their strategy to enhance your product for the better service of your customers.

3. **Use target Adverts**

   Using target adverts such as Facebook and Google, though very cheap, can go places.

   Most commercial adverts in the real world, though well planned and executed, can reach people randomly, such as people who come across billboards at crossroads or read daily or weekly publications. However, targeted ads are more likely to find the people who are in need of your product based on demographic characteristics. By using a target ad: Google pay per click or Pay per impression method, you can know your conversion to sales ratio.

4. **Smart Social Media**

Having a Social Media presence helps you keep your customers. Therefore you need to put in extra effort on Facebook, Twitter and Instagram since these Social Media maintain your presence on their platform

Most businesses use their account to promote their corporate office, smart social media managers plan for essential posts, link to attractive articles, answer customer questions when appropriate and try to give online visitors the impression that they care for their online needs. By adhering to all of the above, you retain their customs by giving users new ways to use your products and assist in solving customers' problems whenever they arise.

5. **Respond to Every Email, Tweet, Phone Call and Facebook Comment**

You must give a positive response to every complaint or comment from the customer by any official in your office. Answer all calls, show that you care for your reading audience, and fix their problems as they come in, they will be happy to associate with you.

6. Affiliate Marketing

Affiliate Marketing is where you are rewarded by a business through your marketing efforts for bringing in a visitor or a customer to the business. But despite its manifest advantages, it is still overlooked by many companies. Affiliate marketing is highly effective in raising brands awareness and promoting a business.

With so many affiliate networks available, which function on a PPC (Pay per Click) or PPA (Pay per Action) basis, it has never been better to find your product being promoted by fitting publishers.

7. Establish Trust In Your Community: Publish User Reviews, Syndicate Articles

With a great number of competing businesses, each struggling to be seen or establish trust, it is never easy to stand out and grow a substantial following. To be trusted, companies must in the first place establish trust amongst the people.

Since about 89 per cent of consumers trust online reviews as much as personal recommendations, it is only a good idea to start publishing user reviews and sending samples of your product for trusted bloggers to review.

With your publishing company beginning to grow, initiate inserting in-house content in big websites that publish collective content, like Forbes, FT, Fast Company and Inc. Always use your real name since people respond more to a human being than to a company.

8. Connect with The Right Influencers

Dealing with big industry players can be a very effective way to gain a wider audience share base. The simple truth is that if you can get the attention of an industry thought leader, a mentor or an influencer, you are likely to capture their fans and friends and also create trust and credibility.

Connect to relevant bloggers or entrepreneurs at public functions or even over Twitter, send them significant and appealing blog content that might arouse their interest, and don't forget – always be a human being, not just a business entity.

9. Post Relevant Content On Blogs

Make it a practice to constantly and industriously publishing appropriate and unique blog content constantly helps keep your company in the limelight, but it also helps potential customers get to know your publishing company and what stuff it is made of.

The content is better not be self-promotional but put forward into context why your product or service is an essential read, propose the best ways to resolve industry-related problems that arise in the everyday lives of your target audience, impart some useful words of wisdom, and in the main, encourage people to share your point of view.

If you cannot deploy enough resources or get writers to build a constant stream of content for your blog, contract it out to online freelancers.

10. Craft an Engaging Newsletter to Encourage Leads

One of the most challenging aspects of online marketing is acquiring leads. Usually, it involves the analysis of customer demographics and social media activity, advertising and conducting online surveys and updating user data from time to time.

But, new companies are emerging that appear to make the process of lead generation easy, possibly doing the work for you.

Therefore, the ball is in your court to nurture your prospects with personalized email newsletters, A/B test promotional blitz. Make use of the data to make your efforts more efficient and your promotions effective.

CHAPTER 9: Marketing Your Publishing Business

Word of mouth recommendation is still considered to be one of the most powerful ways to market a good product. It is free, credible, and a high viral resource that put flavor to your efforts in creating awareness and buzzes about your work.

Your efforts to make the word of mouth marketing to work is an excellent book that adds value to lives of potential readers and a means of getting the book into the hands of relevant people that will spread the gospel.

Does it sound simple? Yes, it does. The idea is simple but the implementation requires enormous time and effort to carry it out, especially at the initial stage.

But, with good planning, you'll get to that tipping point where your fans will become your advocates in great numbers that will impact on your book sales.

Getting Started

It makes sense to start to plan and execute your marketing strategies well before you put pen to paper in readiness for your book. Ample time is required to build relationships, learn your potential readers' behavioural needs and fashion a base of rabid fans that are thirst for more.

So everything boils down to growing your readership as you write your book, and when it's time to commercialize it, you'll already have an eager audience in the waiting.

The next step you take is all about getting your work noticed and shared by the relevant people that will serve as unpaid salespeople. But don't forget these few key points:

- Focus more on creating awareness rather than selling. You must work to help those who can benefit from your book, find it.

- Be prepared for the marketing and promotion of your book. Even if you choose to contract out the promotion of your book, its success depends on you taking action.

- Marketing and promotion is just an extension of your author platform. For the highest impact, combine the marketing strategies below with the actions you take to build your platform.

CHAPTER 10: Marketing Your Publishing Company

Focus on quality customers

Aim at building tight-knit group of rock-solid fans, and good results will be achieved. If you have 20,000 Facebook followers but only a handful of them pay attention to you and your message, you are unlikely to achieve good results. It means, therefore, to build a brand, business or product, you need a @tribe" of about 1,500 people to spread the word across platforms.

Get your groundwork done.

Before any form of an advert campaign, you must be media-ready. This, in essence, means that you have a well-defined target audience, media message, news hooks, professional author image, professional book cover, etc. It makes no sense inviting a book reviewer or reporter asking for media coverage when in fact you have not done a solid groundwork.

Get a good website with some content (a blog)!

Take out a blogging schedule for Tuesdays and Saturdays, or Mondays, Wednesdays and Fridays, etc., and get writers to write good content to be scheduled in advance. You are more likely to be too busy as the date for the book release draws close, so get things done ahead of time.

Be sure you know how to use social media properly.

If you are not well-grounded on social media, try spending up to 40+ minutes on social media sites every other day, and make sure you are conversant on how to use them effectively. Connect with others, and comment on others' posts with helpful insights. Provide valuable information, answer questions, and give out food for thought. Keep your marketing message at the back of your mind. Be ready to write tweets which will trigger re-actions from others and they will want to re-tweet which provides people with food for thought. If you can be humorous too, that's an added value!

Don't be afraid to give stuff away for free.

People love gifts. Write a quality "how-to" or short story that might interest your target readers and offer it for free on your site. Request for readers email addresses in exchange, and you'll have an amazing list of people to connect when your book is launched or when you are planning an event. The email addresses garnered will be one of your most valuable assets in the foreseeable future.

Provide advance review copies (ARCs/ Galleys) in your budget.

If possible, you should have a budget, but if you don't mail out e-copies of your book to sites and reviewers that will be glad to accept digital copies. Reviewers are always willing to receive books that are yet to be available to the public.

Try to get blurbs (a.k.a endorsements) for your book.

Blow it big. Solicit from other authors you have high regard for or admire to endorse your book, be bold and don't be shy about it! Other authors are always willing, supportive and helpful to authors especially up-coming ones. Be ready to meet them, you will be glad you did. They are real people indeed!

Organize your launch weeks well in advance.

You have so many things you can do on launch week to make things take off with a bang, but most of them need to be planned if you desire to achieve your goal. There is a catalogue of things you need to start putting together/procuring such as a blog tour, inviting friends & family to a signing, contacting book groups, publishing press releases, organizing talks with local interest groups, etc.

Write relevant feature articles for publication in local or niche prints.

Prepare articles for the print media well in advance, because a 3 month lead time is needed, so bear this in mind. It is possible to submit stories or articles to your alumni magazine, community newspaper, or a specialized magazine regarding your book release.

CHAPTER 11: Tips On Marketing Your Publishing Company

1. Discover your potential target audience. This is an important step to take in the promotion and marketing of your book, get it well, it eases the process but getting things muddled up, you have a long way to go. Learn about who the book appeals to, understand their behavioural pattern, and reach out where they are – online and offline.

2.Determine your budget. You much include in your budget every marketing cost you are able and willing to spend in marketing and promoting your book?

3. Craft a marketing plan. This step is very important so don't skip it. Layout your marketing strategies and time of implementation. What is your time allocation for implementation of your book marketing strategies? What are your marketing tactics, the goals you want to achieve and what are your measurement metrics?

4. Collaborate: Get connected using your book's theme and location. Collaborate with Google, companies, businesses, organizations, and other industry experts that you can approach for joint marketing ventures.

7. Build your email list. Request for subscription, and show them why it is going to make sense for them by providing outstanding content. Make use of your list wisely to generate and build buzz for your commercial launch. Engage your fans and potential subscribers early and keep them updated regularly, and ask them for comment so they become part of the successful result of your book.

9. Make your book tie up to trending topics. Provide interesting articles that relate your book topic or genre to current popular interests. These articles should be generated regularly.

10. Schedule social media. Plan and come up with what you want to share with the social

media. Share your profile on Twitter, Facebook, Google+, LinkedIn, etc. Choose the most opportune time for reaching the vast majority of people with Tweriod, Sprout Social and Buffer.

11. Promote your e-book for free. Search for free sites and use them to promote your e-book.

12. Provide a portion of the book for free for on-line reading: Use Goodreads to set up an online giveaway. Or try a member giveaway at Library Thing.

13. Time your release. Tie the announcement of your new book with significant news or other action-packed events, blockbuster movie or trade show.

14. Generate readers guide towards the end of your book. Get readers to know that your book has in place a useful discussion guide at the end, with the help of your book's description.

18. Provide a professional image of the author. Use this photo on all your social media platforms, also at your site, and at the end of your book. Use your author bio in addition, on all your print materials.

19. Send for publication press releases. Publish a press release that will include sufficient and significant information to enable a reporter or blogger to appreciate the news value of your story. Ensure it is clear the story you are telling, the cogent reason why the reader of the press release should be concerned, and where more information is provided if they want to have more information.

CHAPTER 12: Pitfalls to Avoid in Publishing

Although writing a book can be tremendously rewarding, a book is rather a complex piece of work. Putting one together is no easy task. To be successful, authors must try to avoid some common pitfalls.

1. Insufficient time and effort

Having to commit oneself to too many projects at a time is never good for anyone. Writing a book is a significant creative undertaking and should be given sufficient time and energy. Before you start writing a book, figure out how much time you can focus on your book. Determine in advance how many words or chapters you need and then agree on how fast you write. Do you consider hiring a ghostwriter, and to what extent can you engage yourself to the book development process? Give yourself an honest answer, so that you can provide yourself with an accurate appraisal for how long it will take you to write the book, from start to finish.

If you have more than you can chew for the moment, it might be best to suspend the idea of writing a book until a better time.

2. Inadequate funds to cover development costs

The vast majority of authors prefer the traditional publishing contract, with an upfront payment and publicity and public relations being paid for as when due. Different types of books attract different requirements from companies

For example, a non-fiction book will usually need an outline, the idea and three written chapters.

On the other hand, you can go for self-publishing. Never you forget that you are likely to need to hire editors and others with specialist knowledge to consult with through the process.

3. Weak network and community

We are in the digital age so you consider your social media presence, your website traffic and the number you are having in your email list. It is easy to measure, so be wary of it. When you send your book to publishers, the more followers/fans you have the better-negotiating advantage you have..

If however, you want to tow the self-publishing path, you must have a pre-established audience if you want to get firmly established immediately after the book release, since a substantial audience from the very beginning puts you on fast route for market success.

4. Weak market positioning

Imagine your book to be a product serving a defined market and find out its true position. Is it serving unsatisfied demand and what is the competition in the industry like? Research the market using secondary data market reports and estimate how the book will sell when launched. Think about building a focus group to show what people should be thinking in terms of their likes or dislikes about your potential book.

5. Look-alike position

If there is already established competition in your area of speciality, your book must offer a distinct advantage over the existing books. The book must stand out, and cannot seem like another copycat, because distinctiveness in a competitive marketplace is crucial.

6.Weak marketing and PR strategy

Having established a solid PR and marketing strategy early in the process allows you to plan from the beginning.

Strong promotion strategy for a new book is essential. When you pitch, agents and publishers may like to know the composition of your target audience and the reasons why your book will appeal to them.

If you undertake self-publishing, you must plan if you want to make a success out of your venture. Many authors are not comfortable with marketing as it's a completely different area of its own. If resources abound, it is advisable to invest in a book publicist or a marketing company, and that could be a big relieve and make all the difference

CHAPTER 13: How to Expand Your Publishing Business

a. Market penetration

This strategy is based on expanding sales from existing products in existing markets. There are several ways in which this can be achieved. The publishing company can increase the customers' book readership. Alternatively, market penetration can be achieved by attacking competitors' market share through, for example, heavy promotion, intensive distribution, and price discounts.

b. Market development

This strategy for growth involves entering new channels of distribution and/or new markets or new segments with existing books. For example, a publishing company may achieve growth by attacking new market segments, developing new markets. With this strategy, proposed new channels and new markets must be carefully assessed concerning attractiveness, and in particular the extent to which the company can match the requirements for success in the new markets.

c. Product development

This strategy brings new product, either by acquiring another publishing company or fussing with another publishing business and launching its books in existing market. Sometimes it may take the shape of improving existing products or an extension to the existing product range, such as additional chapters or different packaging, but it also may involve completely new products for the same market.

d. Diversification (new products for new markets)

This strategy for growth involves developing and launching new products for sale in new markets. This may be deceptively simple since it is potentially the riskiest and dangerous path open to any publishing company. The pitfalls are many since the ground is usually completely unknown to the exploring company.

Yet it can also be a rewarding path to tread. For some companies, it may indeed be the only way to grow. Writing completely a different book for a different audience may be the only path to growth.

However, in real terms, you can grow your book publishing in the following ways:

1. Use Metadata to Sell More Books

The use of Metadata by authors to differentiate their e-book from the crowd cannot be emphasized. Metadata is the piece of information such as the book title, book's author, book description, genre, etc. This information is needed when you upload a book to a publishing platform.

Devote ample time to fill in the metadata information since this is what will enhance the chances of your e-book appear in Google search, Amazon search, Goodreads search, etc.

2. Upgrade Your Marketing Efforts with 3D Video Mockups

Placeit lets indie writers and self-published authors produce videos to market books and e-books without hassle, as well as book cover mockups. On top of it, you don't need video editing skills to produce a video. It takes just a few seconds to create a video. It is as simple as that.

Writers today use 3D Book Video Mockups to engage people's attention in competitive environments such as Facebook Groups or Instagram.

3. Getting Media Coverage (Press) For Your Book

It may not be easy to have the national press or even the local press discussing your book when you are just coming into the publishing industry for the first time. You can get access to the people from the press once you are known as an author who has written many books, with a proven track record. So aim for the local newspaper and magazines, podcast interview and niche blogs, etc. Be involved in others' book launch, book fairs and other cultural events.

4. Talk to Top Book Reviewers

When your book is complete, pick a reviewer that is accessible and is conversant with your genre. A book reviewer improves on the book and promotes your book's sales. Getting positive reviews helps in the promotion of your book to readers.

5. Book Price vs Sales

Price is the only element of the marketing mix that brings in income, other elements have cost. Set the price right and you make sales, but when you choose the wrong price, you may lose everything. In choosing the right price, anything from $1.99 to $9.99 is an affordable price for your book. You are the only one who can determine the price of your book because you know how much you put in the production and how much your book is worth.

But you should consider the following when pricing your ebook:

– What competitors from your genre are charging for their books.
– The volume of your book. It's fair to charge more for a book of greater volume..

6. Personal Branding Management

Your readers must know what you stand for; your values, interest, passion, and rationale. Be yourself, true authenticity is what readers cherish. Be yourself and provide to your audience all they need to know about yourself to connect with them. Be consistent with the message you share in the Social Media, blog posts, your bio, or real-life communications.

7. What About Book Co-Promotion?

Another book marketing tip that works very well is Co-promotion, it's a brilliant tactic. Collaborate with a fellow indie writer who needs the same assistant as you do. You will want to discuss with your collaborators and co-promoters about how you both can make the most of the opportunity; determine regularity, scene, position, message, etc.

It is possible also to support one another's book along with other books from your peers of the same genre inside blog posts

CHAPTER 14: Establishing Your Brand

Publishing house branding strategy has not been well packaged over the years and the topic has been in the public discourse among industry experts for a while now. Any publishing company who is developing a brand must, first of all, seek identity of the author. More than half of book buyers have some knowledge of the publisher's brands but only a tiny number of book buyers questioned felt that the imprint influences their purchases. With this revelation, it shows that publishers have woefully failed in branding themselves.

How can the publishers rectify this anomaly when the vast majority of book buyers, and indeed 96% of a multi-billion-dollar industry's consumers are not influenced by the brand when they make their purchase? Something needs to be done to ensure that publishers not only connect to the vast majority of consumers but also make themselves relevant elements of an accelerating digital world.

Two of the most common ways that have been used by publishers in branding are through the individual author, and more recently, through using social media marketing to reach to consumers. Both of them have proved effective to a certain degree, but they cannot be seen as a panacea for solving the branding problems.

Author Branding

In a way publishers have customarily used branding to raise up the status of individual authors, fashioning out a brand originated on the standing of individual products. In this case, readers become followers of a particular writer of a book or series of books, and they want to read more. The market for the book/s becomes a captive audience and the authors of such books are ranked high in the industry.

CHAPTER 15: Social Media Marketing and Digital Technology

Another way that publishers are trying to reach out to consumers is through social media marketing. To do well, however, a publishing house must be able to effectively manage its brand, in addition to that of its authors and products. Social media is now the marketing tool that will affect this connection of the target audience, boost in importance for marketing and branding very shortly. Consequently, it has become an essential requirement for a publisher what its salt to have a website, a Twitter feed, an Instagram account or Facebook page. Recent studies were done on how effective the social media marketing has become showed that social media offerings that are linked to publishing products do indeed increase the probability of customers buying products — without due regard whether the author, publisher were the subject for branding.

Other ways to build a reputation as an author/publisher that can probably be linked to your brand include the following:

1. Creating Quality Content

Content creation is one of the best ways of becoming a recognized expert. There is no way you can be known for your ideas alone unless you share it publicly.

2. Social Proof

Social proof means your credibility. What do you possess that is going to get people to know you and take you seriously? In what way can you show that you know what you're talking about and that your ideas will work?

3. Your Network

Your network is the people that surround you. You are judged by your associations. Your network can probably be your idea's advocates.

How To Hire The Right Assistance

As an author and/or book publisher, you will reach a point in your business when you either need to outsource because you need skills you do not have or you want to free up your time.

Some authors would prefer to work alone but a time will come when they cannot cope –either because of work overload or because specialist knowledge is required. In these circumstances, a virtual assistant is needed to do any or some of the following:

- **Book formatting**   This covers eBook, hardcover and paperback

- **Editing** – All aspects of editing are covered.

- **Book descriptions** – This is a sales pitch to the reader listing the reasons they should buy your book. It is a sales gimmick that gets readers to see that the book is for them and make a purchase.

- **Publishing** – This is the aspect that gets the book published both eBook and paperback.

- **Universal Book Links** – Provides you with universal book links that allow you to use one link for your book that will take your customers to their preferred purchasing platform regardless of their location

- **Publisher Rocket Tasks** – Can provide Publisher Rocket, together with Amazon keywords and categories for your book.

- **Ghostwriting** – Ghostwriters write articles, speeches, books, blog posts, email newsletter, web copy and is not credited with such works.

CHAPTER 16: Summary of The Procedure for Recruitment and Selection of Virtual Assistant

i. A staff requisitions form- This is required to be completed by the publisher.

ii. Advertisement is placed.

iii. Shortlist is drawn up and interview is arranged

iv. References – this can be taken up before the interview and used to determine the final selection at the interview.

v. Interviews are conducted including tests for specific skill

vi. Medical examinations are taken

vii. Unsuccessful candidates are notified.

viii. Successful candidates are informed and company records updated.

ix. Induction and training are arranged.

CHAPTER 17: Best Locations for Publishing Business

With the advent of the digital revolution, where a publishing company is located doesn't matter anymore. A publisher who concentrates on e-books can be located anywhere while those who publish hard copy, in so far the marketing is not done by the author can also be located anywhere of its choice.

However, there are cities in the United States that are built for business and businesses of different types thrive there. For a publishing company, it makes no difference. The following cities, in descending order have ranked high for existing business and business start-ups according to a survey conducted by CNBC Metro 20

1. Austin, Texas

2. Provo, Utah

3. Washington DC

4. Denver

5. Charlotte, North Carolina

6. Houston

7. Ogden, Utah

8. Dallas

9. Des Moines, Lowa

10. San Antonio

11. Richmond, Virginia

12. McAllen, Texas

13. Colorado Springs, Colorado

And so on.

Conclusion

Publishing is mainly a commercial undertaking, with publishers working to sustain the business and make a reasonable profit. It is the activity of producing information, literature, software, music, and other content available to the public for free or for sale. Traditionally, the term publishing refers to the production, distribution of printed materials such as newspapers, books, and magazines. But in an age of digital revolution, the scope has widened greatly to include electronic publishing such as websites, blogs, e-books, academic journals, micro-publishing, video game publishing and the like. It is not a business for the unserious people and you to excel in publishing, you must demonstrate that you have the passion for writing, you must have a vision, team leadership, imagination and the ability to work with both commercial and creative insight. The mixture of these aspects forms the fundamental challenge of publishing.

Publishing may be conducted as a commercial, private, social, community, or public activity. The commercial publishing industry has expanded greatly and ranges from large multinational conglomerates to medium and small independents. What makes every publishing business big is that it has various divisions ranging from trade/retail publishing of fiction and non-fiction, academic, scientific and educational publishing. So no matter what you are publishing and, your area of specialisation, and no matter how small you think you are, you must create all the divisions and stages necessary for your final product to come out successful. The stages may include the following:

- Determine why you want to publish a book.

- Put it into writing.

- Seek feedback about your proposed book.

- Select the name of your book or title.

- Engage a good book editor.

- Create and design an attractive book cover

- Set up your Kindle Direct Publishing Account.

- Format and upload your book for publication.

Note: This is just one aspect, other publishers may print their work and organise the promotion and distribution of it.